Doing it Differently

Doing it Differently

*An empowering approach to
thriving through* **Breast Cancer**

PATRYCE SHEPPARD

DEDICATION

In honor of the late Letitia Slater Daniel, you fought a good fight. Thank you for sharing your love, your light, and your journey with all of us. We love you.

This book is also dedicated to each of the one woman in eight who will have her own moments of Discovery and Diagnosis. It is for them as they journey from newly diagnosed patient to survivor, living and crafting their story each step of the way. They will become a blessing to the world, reaching their hands to the women who come behind them. And it is dedicated to all who walk alongside us on this journey, without whom we might never discover our Destiny.

CONTENTS

Dedication.. v

How to Use this Book.. ix

Introduction 1

Dot #1: Discovery... 9

Dot #2: Diagnosis 19

Dot #3: Declaration 27

Dot #4: Documentation.. 33

Dot #5: Doctors.. 45

Dot #6: Dosage... 47

Dot #7: Disclosure 59

Dot #8: Donors... 67

Dot #9: Development 81

Dot #10: Destiny 83

Conclusion 85

Acknowledgments 87

About the Author.. 91

HOW TO USE THIS BOOK

This book works as an interactive set with an accompanying workbook and journal. Because breast cancer is a tumultuous journey, and often one that does not go in a straight line, this book works as a series of guideposts—what I call "dots"—that will help organize and order your experience into a meaningful opportunity for growth.

Each chapter has a series of questions that can be found in the workbook. As you finish reading each chapter, you will see a giant dot at the bottom of the page (as illustrated below) that indicates the chapter has ended and it is time to visit the workbook. There are pages at the back of the book for your insights and notes.

Because the journey can unfold in cycles, spirals, and reiterations, you may want to revisit one or more of the workbook sections over time to reflect on new experiences that accompany the relevant theme (or dot) from this book, or to deepen your contemplations as you gain more perspective.

The companion journal is meant to be a resource you can take with you and record your thoughts, feelings, and experiences at any point. You can purchase the workbook, journal, and Survivor Kit on my website www.doingitdifferentlybook.com. The website also offers additional resources and other materials to support, empower, inspire and motivate you in *doing it differently* as we build a community for survivors at every stage of our journey.

Because we are creating a community of survivors, I also invite you to join the Facebook Group Breast Cancer Survivors Doing It Differently. We read the book, document in our journals, complete the workbooks, and enthusiastically welcome and support newly diagnosed women together.

INTRODUCTION

> *You can't connect the dots looking forward;*
> *you can only connect them looking backwards.*

- Steve Jobs

Are you familiar with the phrase "Hindsight is 20/20," referring to looking back and reflecting on things from the past, with 20/20 being perfect vision? It speaks to the idea that it is easy for one to have all the right answers, know the perfect steps to take and be totally knowledgeable about something after the fact. Many times, we experience moments after a devastation, tragedy, loss, or difficult time in our lives. We may go through the experience being negative, feeling sad, or behaving uncharacteristic of ourselves. After the storm, we look back and realize it wasn't as bad as it seemed or be surprised that we even survived. Regretfully, we have Hindsight moments, vowing to *doing it differently,* if there is a next time. So, instead of having those moments, what if we decided to take a breath, open our hearts, shift our mindsets, and look at our current situation from a positive perspective. Image the possibilities.

The focus of this book is to empower you to change your mindset, so you are more intentional about words, thoughts, and actions. What if we thought positively at the beginning? How would we feel? What would that situation or outcome look like? The possibilities are endless.

Believe it or not this book is not about breast cancer. It is about having a paradigm shift, so you get different results, whatever your current situation. This book is, however, tied to my breast cancer journey, as I share with you my many breakthroughs and the approach I used from Diagnosis to Destiny.

Have you ever had a moment in your life where you wish the light at the end of the tunnel would be at the beginning? A moment where you did not have to face any darkness at all and could have the light you desired right from the get-go? Who wouldn't want that? Who would deliberately say sign me up for the hard road please, if an easier, less stressful, less painful path is available as a choice?

As I look back on my breast cancer journey, or as I like to call it, my character journey, there are some dots, honestly, that I could not foresee connecting at all, no matter what someone told me. My breast cancer journey was a tough one, as it probably is for so many women. I've yet to come across a breast cancer journey that I've heard about that didn't have tears, pain, agony, and moments of despair. This Steve Jobs quote, however, puts in perspective the many moments that started out as despair, then propelled me to my Destiny.

I know it sounds weird to say, something that no one would wish on their worst enemy, would lead to a life of purpose and Destiny, but that is what you are about to read. This book is a dot along the journey that I could never have connected. The last thing I expected to be was an author, but there are moments along the journey that if you saw them, you would know the possibility of this book was inevitable.

My name is Patryce Sheppard, I am a thriving breast cancer survivor. I would like to share with you that you, too, are a survivor. Even if you do not feel like you are at your best right now or going through thoughts of disbelief, depression, and devastation, I want you to know that you are a survivor, so right now hold your head high and shout I AM A SURVIVOR!!! I remember the first time someone told me, I was a breast cancer survivor. It was during an interview on a radio show in October, Breast Cancer Awareness Month. At the time I was still receiving chemotherapy (chemo). One of the listeners called in to congratulate me on being a survivor. In that very moment, I embraced it, immediately realizing that I was victorious and did not have to wait for the completion of chemo or radiation therapy to ring the celebratory bell to declare that victory. I could declare victory now, and I did! You see, every single day that you are alive with breast cancer, you are a survivor and winning the battle.

My breast cancer journey was my biggest challenge ever, and it may be the same for you too. One of the most difficult parts of the journey is knowing how to navigate it, especially when you may not have a blueprint or someone who has walked in your shoes to guide you. It's easier to find success when there is a model you can emulate, but what happens when that does not exist? What happens when you do not have someone who can say, "I've walked miles in your shoes?" What happens when you can't find someone who can relate to the breaking news, that will cause major changes in your life? What happens when you are at home all alone and have no one to pick up the phone and talk to and be completely vulnerable with?

That is why I wrote this book. Throughout my breast cancer journey, from the day of Discovery to Diagnosis, to meeting Doctors and going through treatments, I needed a person, or so I thought. I needed someone who had walked the path that I was on. I was fortunate to have help all around me, from my very supportive and loving family: mom and dad, son, brother, aunts, and cousins. Several girlfriends from church were always there for me too. Dear friends from my hometown of Chicago called often, some even flew in. Although they were ready and willing to step in when needed, I still felt alone. I remember someone once saying, they were in a room full of people, felt alone, but never understood how that was possible. How can you be in a room with hundreds of people and feel alone? Going through this journey, I finally understood exactly what that feeling was all about. It was not that no one was around, it was that no one was around who could fully understand where I was mentally, what I was feeling physically, and how challenging it was to remain positive emotionally, without all the hope in my spirit being drained by this diagnosis.

I was desperate for someone who could articulate what I was going through every step of the way. I wanted not just a play-by-play, but also those deleted files that didn't make the final cut of the documentary or television show. I needed to hear the story about not being able to have the strength to go to the bathroom, so you used it right then and there in your bed, laying in your waste, screaming in the midst of your tears, how could this be me? I was desperate for someone to share with me the idea of what hope, faith, and love looked like in the presence of devastation. All these questions, yet no one I could ask.

As I continued to search for this person—and so do many others like me—I realized we weren't looking for a person, what we needed was THIS BOOK, by an author who didn't just research and read about the journey, but someone who walked the walk and could talk the talk.

We wanted a resource, a guide, an approach, a process that would show us how breast cancer isn't the end of our lives but just the opposite. It is the beginning of the rest of our lives if we decide to see it as such. Breast cancer, while none of us wish for it, is a dot on our journey that leads us to another dot on our personal journey. This book is for you and me. The breast cancer survivor who is determined to not let *this* dot, *this* lump defeat me, but instead see the opportunity to discover the best version of ourselves as we move through the highs and lows of the breast cancer journey and how we can do it differently.

My mom always told me growing up, "Everything is Perfect," and she never said it when things were, well, perfect. She always said it after I finished a complaining session. I would look at her and say, "You cannot be this optimistic. Do you see what I see or what I am going through right now?" We are talking about breast cancer! But I will share with you something that I've learned throughout this journey, and propose to you as a question: What if we did this breast cancer journey differently? What if instead of saying things like "F&*k cancer!" or "Cancer sucks," we said, "Cancer showed me I was more than a conqueror" or "Cancer came to seek, steal, and destroy, but little did it know that I'm a survivor, fighter, and a warrior that cannot be defeated?"

You are about to embark on a journey that will press you towards your Destiny and help you develop into the fullness of all you could ever be. This might seem hard to understand, especially after all the tears you might have cried after your diagnosis, after that terrible moment when you received the confirmation that yes, the lump is malignant and yes, you do have cancer.

Perhaps your doctor just handed you this book after sharing what no doctor ever wishes they had to tell a patient.

I want you to know it is not by accident that you are holding this book. Looking back, my diagnosis is connected to yours, in some way perhaps still unrealized, where you too will be showing others that bad news doesn't have to stay bad. It can propel you to a new you, and you might find that Everything is Perfect too.

In the following chapters of this book, I will share with you the 10 "dots" that will help you frame this journey with breast cancer. It will take you from the day of my Discovery to current day, where I am walking out my Destiny and all the dots connecting them. It is not only a memoir, but also a guide to give you steps to fight this fight differently. It is a process I wish someone would have shared with me in 2017. Now, it is yours and what you can do with it will blow you away.

I cannot wait for you to see the dot of your Destiny that will be revealed as you fight like never before to not only survive but thrive. There is more life to live, more love to give, and you have all it takes for both. Let's start where it begins.

DOT #1: DISCOVERY

My breast cancer journey uncovered the real me. I discovered who I am, who God really is in my life, and I discovered the Word of God, how to break it down and apply it to my daily life.

-Letitia Slater Daniel

Patryce! You're 40 now.

"Do you feel different now that you're 40?"

"How did you celebrate your 40th?"

"What gifts did you get to celebrate your 40th?"

"What advice can you give as a 40-year-old woman?"

These were just some of the many questions I was asked by those close to me as I reached what many would call a milestone birthday. At the time, I really did not know how to answer these questions. The people pleaser in me wanted to come up with a profound answer, something that would be epic and philosophical and possibly make a hallmark card or something, but nothing came to me. I could not just come up with an answer that I thought would do justice to those questions. What I did know, however, was turning 40 was definitely not like turning 24 or 34.

One thing I did notice was my body starting to change. The most drastic change was my body temperature. I felt this every single day. I'm the type of person who is only comfortable sleeping at night when the air conditioning is set between 67-69F and the ceiling fan is on medium, not low or high, just medium. I can remember vividly one day how the temperature in the room was just right, no complaints at all, but then the very next minute, I was sweating bullets like I ran a 5K. If that were not weird enough, the fact that when this happened no one else felt the same, made me pause for a moment. My son made me aware of this when he began complaining that the house was freezing. He was actually wearing sweats in our Texas home and sleeping with multiple blankets on his bed, while his mom felt the room temperature was perfect.

My menstrual cycle was also irregular right around this time. For 29 years, I could count like clockwork, when my cramps would start, the length of the cycle, and how many days before it started over again. Now, it was anything but predictable. It became random, intermittent, irregular, and spontaneous, definitely not fun! On for two months, off for four, then on for one month, off for three. Every 26 days turned to 45 days between cycles and instead of lasting for six days, some lasted one day and others four days.

Because my cycle was so drastically random, I had to make a lot of changes, ensuring I was always prepared. At this point, it was like a pop quiz: I never knew when it was going to come. I purchased three cute makeup bags and stocked them with sanitary products, flushable cleaning wipes, hand soap, and clean underwear. If anyone knows anything about me, I was not going to get caught anywhere in a mess, if you know what I mean. Wherever I went, one of those makeup bags was for sure around. I had one at my desk at work, one in the car, and another in my work bag, just in case I was between my desk and my car and had to take care of business. Those makeup bags were to me like the American Express commercials, "Don't leave home without it." Those bags and I were inseparable.

At my annual ob-gyn appointment, I talked with my doctor about the changes I was experiencing. She assured me I was healthy, and this was just part of a woman's life. She said it was my body preparing for *the change*. Even though I was years away, I learned it doesn't happen all at once but in stages. I was hitting my milestone birthday that no one would let me forget and facing changes that would confirm this new age.

One of the things my doctor asked every time I visited her, year after year: Was I performing self-breast exams? Then, when I turned 40, she asked whether I had scheduled my first mammogram. Now that I was 40, she encouraged me to do them both regularly so that I could get to know my body. She then checked for any lumps or irregularities (while I made the same annual verbal commitment I always made, to start performing self-breast exams). Feeling good after getting confirmation from my doctor that the changes in body temperature and my cycle were normal and just part of the maturing woman's body, I went to my "magical" place: my car.

As a child, I always wanted the big stuff, right, but as I get older, it's the small things that I truly cherish. For me, it is my time in my car by myself. I don't know how you spend your time in your car, maybe it's listening to music, catching up on missed calls, or listening to your favorite podcasts, but it is the silence for me. This is my chance to be alone. My car is an experience. When I am alone in this magical place, I am not a mom, daughter, insurance broker, sister, leader, volunteer, entrepreneur, speaker, author, or anything that someone else demands of me. It is me, myself, and I. So, I wonder, where is that place for you? Do you have one? A place where you can be you without the many roles, titles, and responsibilities that you've taken on over the years? I'm not saying those roles and titles are bad—I love every one of them—but that time to be alone, think, pray, talk to God, and even talk to myself, yes, those are special moments.

Don't get me started about how my magical place comes through when a hectic situation occurs. Life has a way of reminding us everything is not unicorns and rainbows. My place to collect my thoughts, call a timeout, and be disconnected from the demands of the world. If you don't have a place like this, get one! You are valuable and important, having a place to yourself where you can be vulnerable is not a luxury, but a necessity.

One of those private moments in the car had me reflecting on turning 40. I thought about not just the changes that were happening to my body, but the changes that I needed to make in my life. One of those changes that I decided about during suburban rush hour traffic, was honoring my word, in other words, saying what I mean and meaning what I say. For instance, instead of making empty promises as I did with my doctor to perform self-breast exams, schedule my mammogram, or take my health more seriously, I wanted to do it for real…say what I mean and mean what I say. I needed to. This would be THE birthday present. For my friends who asked me what I gifted myself for my 40th birthday, you now know the answer. I decided that every time I came on my cycle, I would perform a self-breast exam. That "honor my word" muscle was going to be worked. I was no longer going to make empty commitments.

Three years later...

It was an extremely hot summer day in Plano, Texas, in July 2017. After working all day, guess what came? Yep, my cycle. It didn't even have the decency to wait until I came home. I was particularly surprised because I had not experienced a cycle in six months, thinking it was completely gone! Packing up my stuff to head home, getting into my magical place, I began thinking about how to spend my evening. My son was at track practice on this day, and thankfully, it was not my turn to drive for the carpool. After practice, they were going out for pizza, so I had a little extra time. Arriving home, I washed my hands, put the salmon in the oven for dinner, made a salad, and decided to take a quick shower. Adhering to my 40th birthday gift to myself, my plan was to perform a self-breast exam, followed by enjoying the delicious meal, and writing in my journal before an early night in bed.

What is this?!

As I moved my soapy hands in a circular motion around my breast, I was stunned as I felt something hard and unfamiliar. The shower ended abruptly as I shouted out loud, "OH MY GOODNESS, is this a lump?" I jumped my soapy body out of the shower, looking into the mirror, feeling the lump as I continued to perform the self-breast exam. *This is a lump, this is a lump, oh my goodness!* Suddenly, I realized I prioritized so many things but with the mammogram, I procrastinated. Here I was: 43 years old and never had a mammogram. Why didn't I listen to my doctor?

Afraid and scared, I dried off and laid in the bed to cry, still rubbing, and feeling the knot in my left breast, when the smoke detector went off, the food in the oven, now ruined. Opening the windows to clear out the smoke I returned to bed still crying. As you can imagine, all kinds of things were racing through my head, it was like being in the twilight zone. Then the phone rang, it was my son. It had only been minutes since discovering the lump in my breast. Now he was asking if he could spend the night with his friend from track practice after pizza. After speaking with his mom, I agreed and felt a sense of relief, knowing he did not need to be home at this time.

Is this cancer? No, this cannot be cancer! No one in my family has cancer. How could I have cancer? Am I about to die? What is going to happen to my son? We live in Texas and our entire family lives in Chicago. Who is going to care for him if something happens to me? Will we have to move back to Chicago, while I'm having treatment? What is going to happen to me? Oh my God, I am too young to die.

With my heart racing, head throbbing, and nose running, I cried myself to sleep, laying on a pillow of worries as I thought in an endless loop, "Oh my goodness, is this really cancer?" That night I cried so much and was so distraught, I woke up sobbing with bloodshot and swollen-shut eyes. After about five hours of pain and agony coupled with the worst headache ever, I went to the bathroom, looked in the mirror and said, "Patryce, calm down and get yourself together!"

GET YOURSELF TOGETHER.

I stood there for a moment, dried my tears, feeling thankful my son was not at home, then went to the one place that brings me peace and comfort, my magical place. It was one o'clock in the morning and I was in no condition to drive, but I didn't need to. Remaining parked, talking out loud to God, and pleading for this not to be cancer, deep down in my heart, I knew it was. Courage and bravery were going to be required. This would be unlike any other experience and would challenge my faith, beliefs, and my strength—physically, mentally, emotionally—and perhaps in ways I could not yet imagine.

Statistically, 1 in 8 women will develop invasive breast cancer over the course of her lifetime. WOW, I had no idea! Additionally, 85% of breast cancer occurs in women who have no family history. Go figure! When you add the fact that 30% of newly diagnosed cancer in women will be breast cancer, and the major risk factors for breast cancer are gender (being a woman) and age (getting older), it's not surprising that 1 in 8 women will have a diagnosis one day.

This is not to scare anyone into scanning the room wondering who is the 1 in 8. This is information, so we are aware of the facts. Sometimes, the shock of thinking, "It can't be me!" can lead to denial, depression, and ultimately delay the treatment we need to overcome this diagnosis.

While writing this book, I learned more and more about the importance of self-breast exams and mammograms and understood why my doctor was so adamant about me regularly having them both. Knowing my body at that level could help my survival rate tremendously. Accordingly, the American Cancer Society says, when breast cancer is detected early, the 5-year relative survival rate is 99%, confirming the fact that self-breast exams and mammograms are so important. Each of us has a Discovery journey. Whether it's a self-breast exam, mammogram, or your own unique Discovery, early detection is key.

Amy Robach (the co-anchor of ABC's *20/20*) revealed in her book that she had her 1st mammogram at age 40. She shared her reluctance to having the exam until Robin Roberts (breast cancer survivor), encouraged her to do it publicly, especially because she could relate to the many women like myself who viewed the show. That mammogram led to Amy's Discovery.

What is your Discovery story? The reluctance of breast cancer survivors to share, leads to what we discussed in the introduction. Remember, we are looking for more people like us, those who didn't just read about what it's like going through breast cancer, the ones that walked the walk and can talk the talk. I was searching for fellow travelers who were living through it or, as Robin Roberts says, thriving through it. For some of us, our fellow travelers are right alongside us, while others look to celebrities and other high-profile personalities who are willing to share the most intimate details of their experiences to help us as we struggle through our own.

The Discovery part of your journey is an excellent place to start if you don't have a clue how best to share your experience. The many survivors like you and me are not looking for experts. What we are looking for is an authentic account from a real person with the raw details included. It is here that we can build community, making this challenging journey towards our destinies much more doable. It's ultimately why you have this book right now. Because I understand the depth of the pain this story sears in us. It drives deep within our souls, and if I can help in the healing process in any way, it might make some of the challenges seem worth it, that are par for the course.

●

DOT #2: DIAGNOSIS

I have the "c" word, is my life over? So many thoughts and emotions. I'm thankful I know God is stronger than cancer!

— *Michelle Iraca-Bowman*

7:00 AM

7:02 AM

7:04 AM

7:06 AM

7:08 AM

You might be wondering why I am posting these times here. What do these times represent? These times represent a woman in the United States being diagnosed with breast cancer. Every two minutes! Sometimes it takes seeing it in this format, to really hit home.

Even more alarming, every 19 seconds globally, a woman is diagnosed with breast cancer. Displaying the time, makes it feel more real, knowing attached to that specific time is a woman. It's not just a number. Attached to the number is a name. Attached to the name are friends and families whose lives are forever changed because of the diagnosis of cancer.

Scary thought, isn't it? It's so scary that many cannot even come to grips to even say the word cancer. Instead, they say the "c" word, almost like when we were children, and we were told not to say the "f" word or the "s" word but we all knew what those words meant.

The time had come for me to find out the diagnosis of my Discovery. Again, in my magical place, I headed over to my primary care physician (PCP). She examined my breast and determined the lump needed to be addressed immediately, I was referred for a mammogram. At age 43, I was going to have my first mammogram. I not only feared the lump and what it meant, I feared getting the mammogram too! Since then, I've heard many people say that having a mammogram is not as bad as one thinks, and I would have to agree, it's not.

If you're nervous about medical procedures, maybe skip this next paragraph. I want to share my surprise and distress about the other diagnostic test I had to undergo after the mammogram. A biopsy. I had a good idea that I would need a mammogram the night I made my Discovery, so that part was no real surprise to me, but the biopsy? That, I was not mentally prepared for. I was introduced to the longest needle I had ever seen in my life. I'm not sharing this to scare you, I'm sharing because the sting of the surprise makes it even scarier than it is. At the end of the needle, there was a clamp to clip and remove a piece of my flesh. None of this was explained when I asked questions and scheduled the appointment. The phone call was for a mammogram and a mammogram only. Combined with fear, this next surprise was harder to take. The nurse said it wouldn't hurt and was just a little uncomfortable. Everyone has a different level of pain tolerance or what they would call "uncomfortable," it was anything but that for me. They explored around my breast with the enormous needle searching for the exact spot, all while asking me to remain still. Tears rolled down my face and I yelped in pain. At that moment, it was clear this was going to be a journey of unexpected twists, turns, and surprises. For starters, that "little uncomfortable" left me sore for almost a week. I do understand, though: it was a pain that was necessary for me to get an accurate diagnosis. Amid my tears, I said I was okay, or at least, I kept telling myself that I was. I took the rest of the day off to ponder all that happened and what was going to happen. I had decisions to make about how to move forward on this journey.

Next on the journey was the weight of the waiting game. I was told it would take a few business days before I would receive the results from my doctor. Filled with anxiety, I waited. The nurse called two days later. With a positive, friendly, and inviting voice, she said, "Ms. Sheppard, we need to make an appointment for you to come to the office so we can discuss your results." At that moment, my stomach tightened, a lump filled my throat, and my breast started aching. I must have asked her in 21 different ways to give me my results, pleading with her to please tell me what they were. She simply replied with her calm voice, "You will need to speak to the doctor, but everything is going to be okay, you're in good hands." Left with no other choice, I gave up trying to get the answer right then and there. With one last dash effort to get the results as soon as possible, I requested an appointment for the following day, and she agreed.

The breast surgeon I went to see was referred to me by another survivor. I was impressed with her credentials, she is professional, top of her class and a world class surgeon. Her reviews, however, were not particularly impressive in the bedside manner category, she wasn't the warm and fuzzy type. My take was, cool, she is an excellent surgeon which is exactly what I was looking for, and it didn't matter that we wouldn't be best buddies and getting mani-pedi's together.

I walked into the waiting room optimistically but was met with a cold vibe, mostly from the temperature in the room, but also compounded by the women who were waiting to be seen. No one was making eye contact, watching television, or talking to one another. Even the people who came with companions were silent. Instead, they sat nervously fidgeting, looking at their nails, or thumbing through magazines. I already expected the bedside manner of the breast surgeon to leave me cold, but I didn't think the overall atmosphere would be the same. After checking in at the registration desk, filling out and returning my forms, I sat back down and immediately began to study the other women in the room, curious, concerned, intrigued.

That one over there, she's in her early 20's, certainly too young for cancer, she must be here just to get a check-up, but hmm, this is the breast surgeon, so the women here either have cancer or are like me, here to get a diagnosis; either way, she is way too young.

That one is a middle-aged woman with a wig and no eyebrows sitting patiently. Out of everyone, she looked the calmest. She probably was going through chemotherapy, given the lack of hair. I wondered how far along she was.

Next is an elderly woman knitting with what appears to be her obviously nervous daughter, whose shaking legs and darting glances gave her away. This might be her mom's first visit or her follow-up visit.

Reading the room was my way of blocking out the reality of what I was about to face. Figuring I could delay my feelings by staring at everyone else (I'm not the only one who does this, right?). A few moments later, when the waiting period was over, I was guided to the examination room to meet my breast surgeon. My first impression was that she knew her stuff—she was very matter of fact and to the point—and indeed, the reviews were correct: she was not the warm and fuzzy type.

"Ms. Sheppard, we reviewed your mammogram and biopsy, which shows a left breast, lower inner quadrant invasive ductal carcinoma, ER-positive, PR-negative, HER-2 negative, and we would like to do another biopsy under your arm to check to see if it has spread to the lymph node. I immediately thought, "ANOTHER ONE OF THOSE IT-DOESN'T-HURT-JUST-A-LITTLE-UNCOMFORTABLE BIOPSIES?!" With tears rolling down my cheeks, all I could hear while she continued to talk was a garble of sounds, like the teacher's "wah wah wah" in the Charlie Brown special. She softly asked me if I had any questions and I returned a soft response, saying, "let's just do the biopsy." All tensed up, this second biopsy was longer and even more painful than the first one. After she was all done, she asked once again if I had any additional questions. I said, "No," and made my way to the front desk to schedule my follow-up appointment.

This is when the gray skies began to form for me. It finally hit me; I was just diagnosed with breast cancer. I numbly walked to the parking lot and sat in my car, it no longer felt magical. For the next hour, I cried my mascara off, feeling absolutely devastated. A devastation that I am sure many women experience during the diagnosis stage or dot.

The moment of diagnosis is when a decision is typically made, although a woman may not realize it. The decision is how to approach your journey, this unexpected future. On one hand, you have the woman who is so terrified by the results of her diagnosis that she does not bother making a follow-up appointment, leaving Doctors to chase her down via phone calls and letters so she returns to the office. This is the path of denial, deciding not to face it, keeping it from everyone, and allowing too much time to pass between the diagnosis appointment and the beginning of treatment.

On the other hand, there is the woman who jumps on top of her health immediately. She makes the next appointment and begins her treatment right away. She is thinking about her Destiny and how, despite the obstacles before her, she will be able to prevail, and not even the "c-word" can hold her back from that.

Both paths are justified. Both paths are legitimate. There is no rubric or answer key when it comes to how one responds to learning their diagnosis. With so much uncertainty and unpredictable moments ahead, it can easily lead to one having their vibe thrown completely off. I also firmly believe, no matter the path we choose to take, it is a decision we get to own. We decide the path and posture as we connect all the dots from Diagnosis to Destiny.

I decided to go deep within my being and reach to the spirit of God that dwells in me to fight for my life. I turned my inclination to deny this diagnosis into a determination to embrace it. Instead of having the journey toward my Destiny halted or derailed, I took the diagnosis as an unlikely detour toward my Destiny. Whatever your beliefs are, please know there is a greater purpose for your life, and it does not end with this diagnosis.

When surfing the web, it's easy to see some of the paths people choose to take. I see the posts and memes on social media such as:

"F&*k cancer!"

"Cancer sucks!"

"I'm going to kick cancer's ass!"

These are natural feelings to have. After all, this thing called cancer has brought about a shift in your life that you could not have expected. Inevitably, it has derailed plans. For many, cancer seems like a rude person who abruptly kicked in your door in the middle of the night, oblivious to your daily routine and plans for your life. The Diagnosis of cancer signifies the end. When I made my Discovery, and amid the many tears, the thought of death did come to mind. How could it not? Cancer can make us feel like our fate has been sealed and not for the better, especially when there is so much about the journey that we don't yet know.

One thing I learned early on, the power of perspective. I dive into this a lot more on the third dot of the 10 dots we will cover in this book, Declaration. I made the decision that my Diagnosis would be the beginning and not the end, understanding that every emotion was legitimate, but I chose not to linger among the negative, demoralizing ones.

There is a version of you yet to be discovered. You've started at the dot of your Discovery, traced the line to your Diagnosis, and now it's time to decide and declare what becomes of your breast cancer journey. I hope you choose to be empowered to doing it differently, to dance in the rain despite the gray skies and approaching storm. We have so much life to live. It's time to fight and not fold. We will prevail and it all begins with how we use our words.

DOT #3: DECLARATION

Not today, not now, not ever will I be defeated.

—Rita Bishop Scaplehorn

Sigmund Freud, known for creating psychoanalysis, once said, "Words have magical power. They can either bring the greatest happiness or the deepest despair." I couldn't agree more. The Good Book says the power of life and death is in the tongue. The words we decide to use matter and truly make the difference, especially when embarking on a journey like fighting through breast cancer.

As we talked about in the last dot, it can be devastating to receive a Diagnosis. That news can rain on the grandest of parades. For me, my Diagnosis was a storm, but I knew what is inevitable...after a storm, rainbows. Knowing that, I am grateful. Dimming my light by complaining about why this happened to me, being negative, and feeling sorry for myself, was not an option. The better option for me was to kick off my shoes and go dancing in the downpour, declaring, believing and knowing, that one day the rainbow would arc through my life. This would be my character journey.

An interesting idea came to me at this point in my life. I believe it can begin to show you how to build a foundation where your breast cancer journey can be your character journey towards your Destiny too. In full transparency, this idea was borne out of great despair. I am by no means a superhero who doesn't experience breakdowns. After all, you should have seen the black streaks of mascara streaming down my cheeks after my second biopsy.

It was 2017 at the time, and I thought, what if I changed my mindset to think positive and operate as if it were 2020? What if I made *doing it differently* a real thing, instead of waiting for my Destiny, walk backward from my Destiny to present time? Perfect opportunity to test my faith, condition my mind with positive thoughts, make decisions about the day, and determine that now was the time for me to walk fully in my healing.

Sitting in my magical place, I wiped my face, got myself together and looked at my image in the rearview mirror, and said:

"You can do this."

"You are strong."

"You are brave."

"You are courageous."

"You can handle it."

"Brave" and "courageous" are words that I had been seeing in Doctors' offices and everywhere. It was like a piece of metal meeting a magnet. Those words and I were attracted to one another. I repeated them over and over again for the next 30 minutes while driving home. I knew what my natural inclinations were and what I normally did in adverse situations, but at this time I chose to do it differently. With the idea that Hindsight is 20/20 and thinking about the hard lessons I learned from the past, this journey was not going to end in a "coulda woulda shoulda"!

I have experienced painful, stressful times in my life, with many of those times, although doing good, being left with the short end of the stick. Can you relate? Bad things happening to good people, not fair, right? Again, my natural inclination when faced with adversity is to be negative and having feelings of anger, sadness, disappointment, resentment, and tons of complaining, behind closed doors. Then here comes my upbeat and cheerful mother shifting my entire mood with her Everything is Perfect conversation. And just like that, I was back to the chipper, enthusiastic, optimistic, and confident person that the world knows and loves.

How do you condition your mind to go from your natural inclination to Everything is Perfect in a snap? Having the power to produce a positive outcome instead of Hindsight is 2020 moments? I am so very blessed to have a Godly mother. All my life, my mom has been planting seeds of wisdom preparing me to reach my Destiny and sharing tools to change the mindset.

There are 3 major ingredients for a mindset change:

1. Affirmations

2. Existing Structures

3. Gratitude

Affirmations, words, or statements you believe in and repeat often. The more you say, read, and think about them, they become a part of who you are. Some say practice makes perfect, I say practice makes permanent. Either way, repetition is key to overcoming negative self-talk in your head. I once read, a negative message heard twice becomes more valid than a positive message heard once. It is imperative that we are mindful and intentional about positive messages that we release from our tongue. My mom always reminds me the subconscious mind doesn't know the difference between reality, dreams, wishes or hopes. It responds to thoughts and feelings; therefore, whatever we feed our subconscious, we manifest in our lives. With that said, we must be intentional with what we let in.

Existing structures are signs, words, and symbols in our environment. They are permanent fixtures. Our subconscious mind automatically understands how to respond, without us having to think about it. One familiar example of an existing structure is a stop sign. Because of repetition, our minds already know, without reading or thinking about the word we automatically STOP. What existing structures are in your environment that you repeatedly see and are subliminal suggestions into your subconscious?

"Everything is Perfect" is about gratitude, being thankful and grateful in everything. When we overcome challenges and celebrate victories, it is imperative to remember every situation and lesson learned, as it bought us exactly where we are today. This is where a lot of the "Hindsight is 20/20" attitude comes in. Have you ever looked back at something that seemed bad, but when you think about it, realize it was a blessing?

On my way home I stopped at the neighborhood Dollar Tree and picked up multicolored sticky notes and a Sharpie. Purchasing enough to make two sets of affirmation cards. One set to stick on my bathroom mirror, the other on the refrigerator door. Each time I walked into the bathroom or kitchen, it was my habit to look at the words and repeat them several times. It reminded me of the television show "Being Mary Jane," where Mary Jane, played by Gabrielle Union, always had sticky notes with quotes to help condition her mind about how powerful she was. I was putting into practice the power of words, and as Freud said, I was bringing my greatest happiness into my life.

This activity subliminally pouring into me, conditioning my mind to see myself as powerful, triumphant, and victorious...leaving no room for negativity. I was putting into practice the power of words and bringing optimism and happiness into my life.

Some of the words I wrote on the sticky notes were:

LIFE	STRENGTH	STRONG
HEAL	COURAGE	
FAITH	PEACE	

In the early days, as a portable tool to always have with me, I wrote the words on the back of business cards. Now, I have a set of 60 portable Affirmation Cards to empower me.

Remember, practice makes permanent but does not happen overnight, and perfection is not a requirement. What is required is an open mind to try, and dedication to see it through. Our thoughts and decisions, as the great motivational speaker Tony Robbins says, help shape our destinies. Saying the affirmations several times a day feeds your subconscious mind. In the moments when you are feeling down, nauseous, losing your hair, and feeling disconnected from the world these life-affirming affirmations are deposits in your spirit, soul, and psyche. You cannot make withdrawals to sustain you through the darkest times without making deposits of resilience, fortitude, strength, gratitude, and positivity.

DOT #4: DOCUMENTATION

I documented my journey so that it may be used as a road map for others on this troubled path.

−Rita Bishop Scaplehorn

The world will never forget when Robin Roberts of *Good Morning America's* (GMA) announced on national television, her breast cancer Diagnosis. Understanding her influence and platform, with love for humanity, she passionately shared her journey. It was inspiring to see her share so openly and fight with such strength, grace, and courage. She received outpouring support and love from her fans and the world.

It was Robin's mother who inspired her to share her story, telling her to "make her mess her message." Speaking about her mom, Robin shared, "She helped show me that there are others who are going to benefit from my story and that the pain and discomfort I am going to go through would be minimal compared to the benefit I could bring to other people."

Remembering Robin sharing her journey resonated with me immensely. Here I was, newly diagnosed with breast cancer, and about to embark on my own journey of healing. Reflecting on the details, it dawned on me how the stories of so many women are more similar than different. In my story and Robin's, we each performed a self-breast exam, found a lump, and then had to undergo a needle biopsy which revealed our early stage of breast cancer. Compound that with the idea that her mother, like my own, was instrumental in supporting us in the journey and providing the encouragement to share our journeys with others. I'm certain the gratitude I have for Robin Roberts and the decision she made to document her journey is appreciated by millions of survivors in the world. I too, am hopeful that my decision to document, will have the same lasting affect as I share this book with the world.

That is what this entire chapter is all about: Documentation.

Before we dive into what documenting is and what it looks like, let's set a few ground rules. First, we can't forget the dot of Declaration we talked about in the previous chapter. We decided to change our mindset and be intentional about the words we use on our journey. It's there we chose to define our journey for ourselves, instead of submitting to what our Diagnosis could mean. This cannot be said enough, it does not mean we don't cry as we make our Declaration. It does not mean that our journey is no longer saturated with tears. What is does mean, however, is our tears won't only be those that come with sadness, but also those that come with great joy. So, let's say it together right now, to make sure we are on the same page. Please declare loudly and boldly: VICTORY OVER CANCER IS MINE!!!

Did you declare it, say it with power and from your heart? So, let's together, say it again: VICTORY OVER CANCER IS MINE!!!

Good! Now, once more for good measure. I want you to declare that nothing—N-O-T-H-I-N-G—is going to stop you from meeting your Destiny. Did you feel that at the core of your being? Did a surge of optimism flow through your body? There is power in the words we use, life-giving or life-taking power. Let's direct our power toward a life affirming Destiny. We are beginning the documentation process and it's always good to start with your best foot forward.

Ever since I can remember, I have enjoyed writing. What I've especially enjoyed is taking notes. Whether it was a conference, webinar, at church, during great conversations, or journaling, I enjoy jotting down my life experiences. Ask anyone who knows me well, they will tell you, I have notebooks and journals everywhere. I indulge this passion with joy when schools are about to begin their fall terms. That is when you can find me at the nearest Marshall's, TJ Maxx, or Tuesday Morning buying journals with motivational quotes. (A little hack for readers: This is the time of year when you can find the best variety and prices! Don't say I never told you!)

As the years have piled up, so have my journals. Every now and then, I pull out an old journal reflecting on the trials, tribulations, and triumphs I've experienced during a particular season in my life. Those journals have recorded profound lessons and raw emotions that provide me with incredible Hindsight. Observing my growth over time by reading and rereading old journals allows me insight to see how my character has developed. Reminding me of when my dad would mark the walls to measure my son's growth over time; this is what journaling does for me.

It was a no brainer for me to journal my breast cancer journey, it's what I do anyway, journal. While I was enduring the second biopsy, I had a feeling this was going to be a long, tough road I was about to travel. I wanted to be intentional about having a collection of my thoughts, ideas, observations, and experiences in real time. I didn't want to imagine just relying on my memories after the fact. My efforts to document the experience were not limited to just writing, but also photographs, paperwork from my visits to Doctors, programs from events I attended, and more. I knew documenting this experience would lead to something extraordinary. How did I know? I declared it.

Making a major leap in my documenting journey: I joined the fourth largest "country" in the world, Facebook. In October 2018, I became a member of that global community to reflect on my growth and, as both Robin and I were advised to do by our mothers, share my story. I wasn't quite sure what that would look like, but I stood by my declarations, my magical words like *faith, heal, strength, courage, hope,* and said this journey will be something powerful for the breast cancer community at large.

If someone had told me, I would then go on to travel the county speaking to educate and advocate for early detection, teach women to perform self-breast exams, answer questions of newly diagnosed women, walk alongside them as a comforting friend through their journeys, and become a published author, at that time I would say no way! But fast forward, I am happy to say you are holding this book in your hand as a product of my documentation.

There is no telling where this journey can take you, so heed my words of advice, let it take you wherever the path unfolds. Be okay with doing it differently. Your Destiny can exceed your wildest dreams, even with a Diagnosis like breast cancer. Or perhaps *because of it.*

Some of you might be thinking, "That is cool for you, Patryce, but you already liked writing so yes, documenting worked for you, but I don't know if I can or should do it. I'm not sure if it's for me." Okay, that's fair. I can totally understand your perspective. Please allow me to share with you the benefits of what documenting can mean for you and for women that will come after us.

The breast cancer journey is not an easy one. I know that is obvious, but it's also not a short journey either. As I reflect on my many journals, there were experiences I could have easily forgotten had I not documented them. The longer the road, the harder it is to remember the moments, especially when that road challenges you to find your inner strength and courage.

Speaking of those hard days, documenting can be an incredible stress reliever. Like my car, my journal was another magical place to be alone, clear my mind, and completely destress. Whether describing a problem, uncovering a solution, or my conversations with God, documenting my experiences helped my life be a little bit easier. On days when I was not feeling myself, it was those journal entries from months past that would remind me of how much I had grown and what I had overcome in a short period of time. It seemed as if the path always seemed shorter looking back, than when I looked forward. Realizing that gave me the strength to push on.

Your documentation allows you to capture your story, jot down your wins, highs and lows, all from your point of view. I remember hearing once that the shortest pencil beats the longest memory. Whether you have the memory of an elephant and never forget anything, or you have a short memory, documenting saves you from missing a moment.

After having a double mastectomy, I returned home prescribed with strong medication causing me to relax and sleep a lot. Friends and family visited often with food, prayer and to sit and visit with me, most of which I don't remember, but thank goodness for a journal. Honestly, I don't actually remember entering data, but just like I said before, practice makes permanent (even in a drowsy state). Weeks later, after the doses were lowered, and some meds eliminated, I joyfully read the entries in my journal. I was so moved by the love, support, food, cards, visits, phone calls, and even *Patryce's Happiness Jar*, a gift from the Women's Ministry at church.

My journal is a timeline sharing my overall growth, steps of my healing, my feelings in the moments, and conversations with myself and God, that I will cherish for many many years to come.

Following are tips to help you jumpstart documenting your own journey. (They are also included in the workbook for reference.)

Tip #1 - K.I.S.S.

Keep It Super Simple. Your documenting process does not have to be an exhibit that will one day be featured in a museum or even in a book like this. Whatever shape documenting takes for you remember, Everything Is Perfect. The focus here is to simply share your thoughts and experiences, so you can reflect on it later, seeing how you've grown in the process. You can choose your own style (full sentences, fragments, or bullet points), whatever flows easier for you and simple.

Tip #2 - Have Fun Shopping.

When shopping for journals, have fun! They come in cool colors, motivational sayings, scriptures, animals, conservative, and blank, whatever your preference, whatever fits, mix or match them, grab a few and purchase them for your journey. I have tons of journals, in every style and color. And you should too.

Now, in the same fun mode, purchase a few pins in bright colors, that coordinate with your journals or your personal sense of style. Make this an outing for FUN!!!

As a woman who appreciates the art of journaling included in the Survivor Kit is a journal, created and designed as a perfect companion to this book and tool to help move you through your process and grow with other women in our community. Also, included in the Survivor Kit is a workbook to assist and empower you too. Please visit my website www.doingitdifferentlybook.com to purchase.

Tip #3 - Write in your own voice.

There is no right or wrong way to journal. It's for you, by you, and about you and it's yours. No need to worry about grammar, punctuation, or proper nouns. In my journals, I write the way I speak in conversation.

Tip #4 - Start with putting the date on top of each page.

This is a great way to see your progress over time. Some days will be easier than others, but when you can see progress, even the tiniest amount, it goes a long way.

Tip #5 - Take your journal with you everywhere.

Waiting at the doctor's office, during your 5-hour chemo session, riding home in the car with a supportive companion, before bed at night, there are so many opportunities to write and document your journey.

Tip #6 - Celebrate every WIN! Gratitude.

Nothing is too small to celebrate. One chemo session down, that's a WIN. Getting good blood results on a weekly basis is a WIN. Someone coming by bringing dinner is a WIN. Getting your strength back is a BIG WIN! Celebrate every good time.

Tip #7 - Commit to writing daily and be consistent so you can have an accurate timeline.

Length is not important. There is no right number of words. It is only for the sake of accuracy and helps you to check in with yourself consistently. Even if you can barely pick up the pen and just make a squiggle, that in itself will be documentation of your fatigue as well as your commitment and effort. Show up everyday!

Some additional things to consider:

Jot down your feelings in the moment (unfiltered).

Remember this is for you and does not have to be shared with anyone if you don't want to. When writing those feelings, do not forget to include your fears, expectations, disappointments, and surprises. All your emotions and feelings are VALID—what we repress, we express, often in unhealthy ways. Do not hold onto these things. Remember, documenting can be your stress reliever.

Photographs.

We shared earlier that documenting is more than journaling. It can also be the collecting of paperwork from your doctor appointments along with pictures, which we strongly suggest you take. Remember, a picture is worth a thousand words, so definitely take advantage of having them.

Some pictures I suggest you take are:

- Appointments.

- Ringing the bell at completion of chemo and radiation therapy.

- Photos with family and friends.

- Photos at therapy and with doctors and nurses.

- Getting a haircut and wearing favorite wigs, scarves, and hats.

- Favorite books you are reading.

- Pretty things that strike your eye, like a flower on hospital grounds, a sunset, or freshly painted fingers and toes.

Other kinds of documentation.

- Positive notes jotted by new friends and health care providers.

- Parking stubs.

- Pressed flowers from bouquets.

- Cards received.

- Hospital pamphlets.

DOT #5: DOCTORS

When a woman is diagnosed with breast cancer, she has to include everyone in on the process, including a positive relationship with doctors.

— *Gigi Vinique*

This journey is a long one and because it is, the right fit and connection with your Doctors is essential. The correct understanding of the roles your Doctors play is necessary, so please ask them questions for clarity. Two-way communication and your participation is also necessary. Your relationship with your Doctors is magical because you both are equally a part of the solution to reach the goals of health and healing.

Trust your Doctors, they are the specialist with your best interest in mind. Your Doctors are your friend. If you have questions, please ask them, not the internet which can be totally confusing, as it does not know or understand all the details of your health.

DOT #6: DOSAGE

> *Understanding chemo is a poison, it's not natural, breaks down your immune system, kills good and bad cells, and after studying the side effects, I'm scared and I'm choosing to trust God and move forward with the process.*
>
> — *Gigi Vinique*

My initial introduction to chemotherapy was from secondhand information, television shows, and Hollywood movies. Later, I met women who shared their personal stories firsthand. It all sounded very scary, and at the time, I was grateful it wasn't happening to me. Fast forward to 2017, I'm sitting in a reclining chair with an IV pole receiving chemo.

For the sake of his book, we will refer to chemo as poison that kills cancer cells. That's a good thing, right? Well, let's be clear, it annihilates good cells too, negatively impacting our immune system. I will share later with you, what I did to counter this impact.

Chemo is not easy but was part of my healing plan. I trusted my Doctors, scheduled my appointments, and jumped in with both feet and faith, for this aspect of my treatment.

The plan from my oncologist was chemo, surgery, then radiation. I was asked to decide rather I wanted a lumpectomy or mastectomy of my left breast. I had time to think about it, sleep on it, and pray. Having the time to decide, I used it to make the decision that was right for me and my life. I wanted to be comfortable and fully involved in the process.

Making sure we are on the same page when I refer to Dosage, what I mean is your course of treatment and medication. This is something our Doctors prescribe, along with the plan of action. This looks different for everyone, as we each begin at different stages, but no matter what the stage, we all have a treatment plan.

My Treatment Plan

In preparation for chemotherapy, a port was installed during outpatient surgery (a minimally invasive surgical procedure, with local anesthesia, some sedation and pain control medicine to take home). Subsequent to inserting the port, 8 rounds of chemo (in other words, 1 session every other week for 16 weeks), with 4 rounds of AC followed by 4 rounds of Taxol (both chemo meds).

What Is A Port

A port is a small disc made of plastic or metal about the size of a quarter, that sits right under the skin. A soft, thin tube called a catheter connects the port to a large vein. The port is inserted under the skin. You can usually bathe, without being concerned with the risk of infection.

Your chemo meds are given through a special needle, fitting right into the port. You can also have blood drawn through it too. A port is easier than inserting an IV, as some people have veins that are difficult to access, like me. The port route allows easy access to the bloodstream, so you get the medicine you need. Without a port, a PICC line (an IV) will need to be used each time you have chemo, with a separate IV line if you require IV fluids or a blood transfusion. Sometimes it takes several attempts to find a good vein. With that said, if you are not a fan of needles, a port is the perfect way to go.

One minor drawback with the port, it leaves a scar on the upper chest where it was inserted. Given what is at stake, and the benefit of having the port, plus Everything Is Perfect, once you ring the celebratory bell at the completion of chemo, you now have a battle scar and something to brag about later.

Healing Process Begins

Similar, to my very first day of school, I walked into the infusion room like a nervous little girl. Eyes wide open and curious, not knowing what to expect. What I knew for sure, was that I should simply be my usual self, smiling brightly and greeting people. A nurse smiled and introduced herself, then walked me to my seat. One smile down, I thought, hoping for many more.

I locked eyes with an interesting woman, my chair sat next to hers. Beaming my pearly whites, I smiled and said "good morning," as she turned and gazed away. Not a word! Perhaps she didn't hear me, I thought, so I spoke a little louder, still smiling and said again "good morning". This time she replied with a growling mumble "good morning", still looking away. In my peripheral vision, she turned her head and looked in my direction. I smiled and said, "it's cold in here, isn't it" and she mumbled, "the nurse usually brings warm blankets", and she did.

Getting comfy in the reclining chair and starting to read my new favorite book, I felt a familiar chill in the air, that had nothing to do with the thermostat. It had everything to do with the energy in the room and the sadness and broken spirits of the patients, observed today. Hopelessness and despair filled the room. Sadly, I thought, this is what death feels like (my eyes begin to water and tear). In my imagination, I was running from the room to my magical place, with my valet parking ticket in my hand. I was snapped back into reality, when the nurse came to check on me and monitor the chemo machine.

Instead of reading my book, I pulled out my Affirmation Cards reading them one by one, knowing the new energy would calm me and protect my vibe. Then, out of nowhere, grumpy woman asked me abruptly, "What are you here for? What kind of cancer do you have?"

Like a deer in headlights, I froze and without hesitation or thinking said, "I DON'T HAVE CANCER!" In Hindsight, my answer was untrue and totally ridiculous, but an unconscious effort to not associate myself with the doom and gloom and heartbreaking brokenness of the patients in the infusion room. She ignored me, then complimented how pretty I was and how fancy I dressed, just to come to treatment. What she did not know, I always leave my house looking "fancy"...smile. She then said, without breathing or blinking, "you know you're going to lose your hair, right?" I was appalled! I knew she was telling the truth, but she could have kept that to herself, and simply smiled and said hello.

In my mind, I went back to the Affirmations that I earlier read, then silently declared that cancer would NOT control me, I WILL CONTROL CANCER. I will lose my hair, by choosing to cut it myself, Period!

Refusing to be aligned with the cold energy in the room, wrapped in my blanket, I grabbed my IV pole and made a mad dash to the ladies room to collect and empower myself by reading the Affirmation Cards, and to breath. Grateful for the silence and powerful words, I was now centered and back to me.

Returning to my seat in the infusion room, I smiled at the grumpy woman while settling myself in the recliner. Opening my journal, I was greeted by colorful sticky notes with more Affirming words. I smiled and again, felt grateful.

I was awakened by a gentle touch on my shoulder and a soft voice. It was the nurse, inquiring about my comfort and checking on the machine. To my surprise, my grumpy friend was gone. I thought, there must be a sleep aid in the chemo meds, as I never even realized that I had fallen asleep. I hope I didn't snore.

Then, out of nowhere, a beautiful smile entered the room belonging to a woman name Tamara Newborn. Another smile! She was wearing the cutest survivor t-shirt and was there for chemo like me. Tamara was upbeat and encouraging, sharing her challenges and victories, telling me that I was a winner too. We became instant friends and still friends today.

After treatment, the nurse placed a medication on my stomach called Neulasta. She said it would auto release in 24 hours. I asked her to take a picture of me, then I took a selfie to tape in my journal.

Just like she said, the Neulasta released, making me so sleepy, I slept like a baby for the next 24 hours. Waking up refreshed, I showered and began my day, journaling. My first entry was a reminder to ask my Oncologist about the Neulasta medication. With so many conversations and new information, I didn't recall having a consultation about the new medicine. So it stood out and I wouldn't forget, I titled the page, Questions to Ask My Doctor on My Next Visit.

Hooray, the Women's Conference at church is finally here. I looked "fancy" and felt great! I enjoyed serving and fellowshipping with guests and friends. It was an amazing event. Happy, smiling and taking pictures, little did I know today would be the last day I would sport my big curly afro.

As everyone's experience is different, please see below a few things I learned regarding chemo and how it affected me:

1. Chemo is cumulative, meaning each treatment builds on the other, symptoms compound, and weakened my body with every treatment. The medication in some cases, affects each person differently.

2. My hair began shedding after the 2nd treatment, I shaved it the same day.

3. Around the 3rd treatment, I started feeling moments of tiredness, pain, and nausea.

4. I learned to listen to my body, rest, and recharge.

The first two rounds of chemo weren't as hard as anticipated. I remember calling my mom with the great news. Round 3, however, kicked my butt; the side effects had me feeling foggy, my body was achy, urine was dark with a foul odor and my body felt like it was breaking down (guess it was working). The game changed swiftly; I was no longer able to drive myself to appointments. I was grateful to the dots Disclosure and Donors, and to my awesome girlfriends for coordinating their schedules and taking turns to accompany me to each of my clinics, I call them chemo buddies. I'm so glad to have shared with them the details of my journey early on, as they were immediately prepared to give support.

Not Your Ordinary Monday

It was Monday afternoon when I first noticed a few strands of hair on my pillow. Immediately, ran to the restroom, stood in front of the mirror, and ran my fingers through my big curly afro, at least 10 strands of hair came out from the root. This was the moment where my Diagnosis dot met and connected to the Dosage dot and reality sank in, MY HAIR!!!

Faced with this reality, I leaned on the sticky notes that were on my mirror. The note that stood out to me was the one I declared, after the statement from the grumpy lady about losing my hair, "cancer will NOT control me, I WILL CONTROL CANCER. I will lose my hair, by choosing to cut it myself, Period!"

I went into the living room where my son was watching football and eating snacks. I showed him my 10 strands of hair, shared my Declaration and told him I was cutting my hair. He smiled, said he understood and agreed with me; I was happy to know my teenage son was okay having a baldheaded mom. Softly sobbing, he took pictures of me cutting my hair.

When done, he laughed and said, "You still look pretty, Mom, but you now need the barbershop!" We had a hardy laugh and I agreed, because plugs and bald spots were all over my head. Such a cherished and most memorable moment.

The next day I went to my son's barber, Kevin. I arrived at a time when he wasn't busy, which gave me time to sit and talk openly with him, as he was my son's barber for years and now a family friend. He shared with me, his mom was a breast cancer survivor and that he understood. Kevin shaved my head and I agreed with my son, I was still his pretty mom. He was now my friend and barber and would call or text to check on me (especially after surgery). We once even had lunch after chemo. The best part ever, is friendship with his mom, Teresa, my pink *sista*.

One thing I learned in this journey that I want to pass on to you, is the importance of having people in your life who have endured the journey themselves or have served as caregivers. That is exactly why I decided to write this book. Make sure you too have a Kevin in your life.

The Regretful Search

I learned a few important lessons like using numbing cream and clearing the bandage over the port for more comfort and less pain. As the nurse injected the medication, something caught my attention. It was a red substance that was going into my IV bag. Curious, I asked her what it was, and she replied it was doxorubicin. She said this is the medicine the grumpy patient was talking about, when she told me I would lose my hair. By now, you know my next move, I entered the name of the med in my journal for later. Once the IV drip started and I was feeling warm and toasty wrapped in blankets, I decided to google the word doxorubicin. Next lesson learned, DON'T GOOGLE, as this medicine is referred to as "red devil" or "red death." Immediately, my heart began to pound, my mouth started to water, and my stomach turned, running faster than the speed of light, I darted with the IV pole to throw up in the bathroom, hoping I'd make it to the toilet and not the floor.

Sick to my stomach, throwing up and crying, right then and there I promised myself to never google again. I wanted no association with treatments or words associated with "devil" or "death", not because I was afraid, but because it was my actions that opened the door for negativity. Collecting myself, I returned to the infusion room and journaled, "NEVER GOOGLE!!!" If, I had questions, I would ask my trustworthy doctor for clarity, not the internet.

What Your Doctors Don't Cover

When it comes to your treatment, there are parts of the process that your Doctors do not cover. It is important you fill in the gap to ensure your healing journey is not missing anything vital.

Nutrition

We talked about chemo being a poison, it kills bad cells, as well as good cells. It does the work to stop the cancer from growing. My Jamaican friend Monica is a health and wellness educator. She kept me company, caring for me like a big sister. I really appreciated her consultations, as they were so valuable. We talked pros and cons of chemotherapy, flushing chemicals from our bodies, boosting our immune systems, and how to feed our bodies from the cellular level with nutrients.

My immune system was weakening, my body was filled with toxic chemicals and my appetite was loss. Monica taught me the benefits of juicing and how to juice. I had no desire for solid foods but juicing feed my body necessary nutrients and cleansed my system of toxins. Some of the benefits are: it helps boost the immune system, absorbs quickly, repairs cells, hydrates, and tastes great! Can you see now, how I was a huge fan of juicing during chemo? Juicing is a low-effort opportunity to consume kale, spinach, parsley, lemon, ginger, celery, cucumber, and green apples in a single green drink. It was far easier for me to drink my fruits and veggies, than it was to eat solid foods during my treatment period.

Mind/Spirit Medication

In my experience, my Doctors covered the body, with prescriptions, recommendations, referrals, chemo, radiation therapy, surgery, and pharmaceuticals. But we are more than just physical beings. We also have our minds and spirits. Remember earlier we talked about Doctors and how they have specialties? Our mind and our spirit must become our field of specialization. This is where sticky notes and journaling come in. Being mindful of what I call our "personal prescription".

Personal Prescription

What is your daily medicine for your mind and spirit? Have you given this much thought? Hopefully by now, you realize the power that lies within us to help overcome this hurdle called breast cancer. Are you regularly reminding yourself of your declarations? Are you using the power of words to help shape your mind with thoughts that heal and restore?

This journey is a fight like no other and is going to require more than you can imagine. Don't fret, you got this! You are a warrior, more than a conqueror. You have strength and courage. You are faithful and ready to fight. These are the daily reminders that allowed me to continue my healing process, even when my Dosage physically wiped me out.

Take a moment to identify what your personal prescription is like, for real. Put this book down, step away, grab hold of your journal, to take inventory and write your personal prescription. Think about it like this, your personal prescription is designed to help you with symptoms you face when going through this journey. Here are a few in the category of mind and spirit: fear, doubt, worry, concern, hopelessness, defeat, despair, dejection, depression, and anger. These are just some symptoms to give you an idea. Got it? We need to know them ahead of time, so when they appear we're prepared and not ready to throw in the towel.

My heartfelt desire is for you to feel POWERFUL, knowing you will not break, as you victoriously meet your Destiny.

DOT #7: DISCLOSURE

Lies and secrets, they are like a cancer in the soul. They eat away what is good and leave only destruction behind.

— Cassandra Clare

When we were younger, my brother Patrick was a BIG wrestling fan. Are you a wrestling fan by any chance? If so, you're going to enjoy this quick trip down memory lane (if not, trust me, you will get the point). Remember Stone Cold Steve Austin? His nickname was the "Texas Rattlesnake", he was a rebel, a person who did things his way, operated alone, and never joined a community or clique in the wrestling circle. His catchphrase is "DTA", meaning Don't Trust Anybody. He never counted on or trusted anyone, feeling they would turn their back and betray him anyway, so why bother? Although he was a famous, household name amongst wrestling fans young and old, I imagine him being an introvert or a very lonely man.

The decision for you to do it alone, can determine the quality of your experience. It can feel like a ton of bricks or a breath of fresh air. Choose wisely. Let's be clear, this is

YOUR decision to make. Understanding, there are people we should not trust with this information, or at least discern when the timing is appropriate to share, but DTA is a recipe for destruction. I made up one for us, how about CTE, in our case, stands for Can't Trust Everyone. You need people on this journey, that goes without saying, but you don't need everyone to know your business. This subject is sensitive in nature, and I honestly had a hard time making the determination of who to disclose to and when, so this, in all honesty, is a Hindsight 20/20 moment for me.

Recently, I posed a question in a breast cancer survivors' group online requesting, what information they wished they had known ahead of time. Of course, the responses were abundant as we all have an absorbent number of questions and are always seeking answers. There was one response, though, that intrigued me. Being transparent, I experienced a situation that I would have never referenced in this book had so many women not responded with this answer. This ah ha moment for me further confirmed the need for a community of women who have walked the walk and can talk the talk, so we understand no part of the journey we are experiencing is in isolation. Take a deep breath, ready, set, go!

The overwhelming response was women did not realize how much negativity they would receive from others while traveling on their journey. The thought that we, us, breast cancer patients, survivors, thrivers are here fighting the battle of our lives and are being met with negativity, absolutely, breaks my heart. I need you to hear me right now: we do not have the energy to fend off naysayers or people who inexplicably cannot comprehend the stakes of the battle we are fighting. When you are faced with this situation, make a mad dash to your magical place collecting your Affirmation cards along the way. Let them eat your dust!

Here's the reason why I am so sensitive about this and why I've dedicated a dot on this topic. Breast cancer attacks all aspects of our being, as I described in the last dot. We cannot take on or do not need another opponent. What we do need, however, is positive energy, love, and support. Having those three ingredients makes it easier for us to be vulnerable and disclose our story.

Keeping Your Diagnosis A Secret.

Think about your situation. Did you want to keep your diagnosis a secret? If so, why? Were you trying to protect others from being burdened with the weight of your diagnosis? Fearing how they would respond? Hearing the "c" word and automatically assuming the "d" word (death)? Or were you protecting yourself? Not ready to accept the diagnosis? Did you need more time to process? Were you afraid of facing your loved ones, unwilling to answer questions, or face their tears and fears?

Deep consequences are attached to keeping this secret, cutting yourself off from the very support needed to see this through from Discovery to Destiny. Another lesson along this character journey I've learned is everything is not what is seems. For instance, solo sports in all actuality are team sports behind the scenes. When Serena Williams plays singles in Tennis, all eyes are on her, but remember who's in the box watching, cheering her on, and providing the support she needs to perform her best, her dad, mom, sisters, husband, and daughter. Disclosing your diagnosis isn't about privacy but positioning yourself within a supportive community to receive the love and support you so desperately need.

Thinking about my team, the group of people who rallied and gathered around to walk alongside me during the toughest days of my life, I feel warm and fuzzy every time. Could not even imagine what my life would have been, without the overwhelming help that I was blessed to receive, and guidance. In the next chapter, when we talk about Donors, you will learn more in detail about building a team. For now, please accept that it is imperative to disclose, even if it is outside your comfort zone, after all, we are, *doing it differently.*

How much to disclose?

Now, after deciding to disclose, the next step was being mindful about how much to share. There was so much to consider. I remember what it was like receiving the information myself, and I considered my feelings before disclosing to others. Giving a play-by-play like a sporting event was not necessary, just enough details to ensure they understood we would be on a journey, and I would need their support. I also made a promise to keep them updated every step of the way.

When to Disclose?

Heads up: I'm not accusing you, I'm talking about me. My mom raised me to be an independent woman, and there are so many others just like me, headstrong, confident, and thinking we can do it all, wearing our tights and capes flapping in the wind. Recalling previous dots, I was alone during Discovery, Diagnosis, and the first few Dosage appointments, not because I had to, I chose to. Family and friends reading this, please accept my humble apologies. I know you would have been right there by my side accompanying me to appointments and being a shoulder to cry on when I was Diagnosed. Attending chemo alone a few times in the beginning, was so unnecessary. No excuses here, although, I would like to share why it took so long for me to disclose. I didn't want anyone feeling sorry for me, and I was embarrassed to ask for help. That sums it up. There is no right or wrong time to disclose this difficult information, I suggest sharing sooner rather than later. I didn't have a plan, and I didn't share with my mom until I was about to have the port inserted right before chemo (shaking my head). The good news is you can learn from my Hindsight 2020 moment and do it differently so your circle can cheer you on and provide support so you can be your best.

Who to Disclose to?

Your diagnosis does not need to be on the front page of the community newspaper. Sharing with the masses will not necessarily bring more support. It is important to use discernment and be mindful of who we are disclosing to.

How do we decide? I suggest, people who always see the glass half full, those optimistic ones. This is who you share with first. Think of them as part of your Dosage. Remember we talked about the treatment/medicine in the last dot, the kind that the doctor does not control? The mind and spirit kind? This would fall under that category. People who speak positive, and see your journey as you do, share your vision for your Destiny, fully onboard.

I know you are probably giving me stink eye, thinking, Patryce, you just admitted telling "Ms. Everything is Perfect" two months after you received your Diagnosis and right before the port surgery. Now you're giving us advice on when to disclose? That's probably what I would be thinking, but we are changing our mindset, right? I have walked the walk so I can talk the talk. I handled mine incorrectly, hope your experience is different and that you commit to *doing it differently.*

Although it took some time, when finally disclosed, I had a plan. Understanding the importance of a powerful team surrounding us, I began to assemble mine. This team of family and friends were focused on the same goals, with embracing love and never any dissension. I am blessed to have the support of other amazing people, who showed up specifically to help me in my healing season. I am forever touched, moved, inspired, and changed, to my core, with the many acts of love, that reminds me of the Golden Rule (do unto others as you would have them do unto you). Those sweet sentiments, are deeply impressed in my heart, causing me to want to give and love so much more. Grateful!

One last nugget. Assign a point person to help with disseminating the news. We are in the conserving-your-energy situation. A trusted family member or close friend who can relay the information is invaluable. Be sure they have enough details to answer questions knowledgably. This is less stressful than your phone ringing and text messages coming in like 40 going north. They are the point person, gatekeeper, and confidant, responsible for getting information to your loved ones and keeping them updated so they aren't left completely in the dark about what is happening with you.

In this dot we talked a lot about me and covered what, how much, when and to whom we should disclose, it's time for us to dive into the next dot in doing your breast cancer journey differently, Donors. Buckle your seatbelts, in this dot we will be looking more closely at you and discussing real issues that may move you out of your comfort zone into a new paradigm shift.

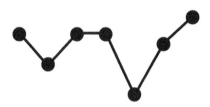

DOT #8: DONORS

This journey is not all about me but allowing others to fulfill their purpose in banding around me and being my support as I fight.

— Lori Hayley

Let me introduce you to my friend Candice Brandt, also known as Candy, but I call her "Candy Cane." At 17 years of age, she was diagnosed with juvenile, or Type 1 diabetes. At age 21, the diagnosis complicated into high blood pressure, which transitioned to chronic kidney failure at the tender age of 37. Her condition were life threatening.

After Candy was Diagnosed with diabetes, there were changes she needed to make, such as increasing her physical activity and monitoring nutrition. Her lack of discipline developed into high blood pressure, accompanied with bad headaches, back pain, and other ailments. Due to weight gain and not adhering to the Dosage her Doctors prescribed, the condition worsened (remember, our Doctors and their Dosage plans are essential components of our healing journey). To cope with pain, Candy used ibuprofen. Not realizing that taking over-the-counter medication combined with disobeying her prescribed Dosage was a recipe for disaster on her kidneys. Working overtime, chronic kidney failure was the result.

You may be wondering, why I started with this section with a Debbie-downer story? What is the point of sharing this, Patryce? Trust me, hang in there, you'll see, Everything is Perfect.

Throughout her illness, Candy experienced many difficult days. Her health took a turn for the worse when she suffered a stroke on a City of Chicago subway train. Can you imagine, at the age of 37 years old, being a single mom of an 8-year-old daughter, and now in a predicament where your life is on the line and wondering how long you're going to live? Sound familiar?

I drew near to Candy, as much as she would allow me.

Candy Cane's journey was anything but easy. At age of 41, she began dialysis, that lasted four long excruciating years. It was hard for her, especially in the beginning. She lost sight in her right eye (due to diabetes), and three times a week went to have her blood cleaned, it was recycled from her body through the machine and back into her body now clean, that is how she described dialysis to me. She would return home weak, in pain, and lay in bed for days with cramps running up and down her body. A few times while having treatment, she lost consciousness because her blood pressure dropped extremely low, thankfully the nurses were able to revive her. The first time this happened, she called me in a frenzy, shaken and afraid, but grateful for another chance at life. I was horrified but knew I couldn't express my feelings, so I listened, and we prayed. During her time on dialysis, I can recall instances where she saw this happen to others, many were revived, but some were not as fortunate. The nurses tried with everything they had in them, when they stopped working and called the ambulance, the patients in the room knew what that meant, the "d" word. This is probably what the grumpy man was referring to on Candy's first visit.

These experiences forced her to adhere to her Doctors Dosage to change her diet, after all, she could only drink 32 ounces of water a day, and if she didn't follow the strict guidelines, she would pay for it at the next dialysis appointment.

Candy's Life Begins to Change

Over the next few months, I began noticing her personality change, she wasn't a sweet Candy Cane she was more like a lemon head, more sour than sweet. Distant, mean, unwelcoming, and very grouchy. She pushed people away, but not me, I'm not the kinda girl you can easily push around. She was bitter, instead of getting better. Nonetheless, I couldn't and wouldn't let my girl go through this alone, so I remained persistent in checking up on her and we set dates to call each other to pray and exchange words of encouragement. What an awesome way to start the day!

Facing an adverse situation, running low on mental and spiritual strength, I was right there to lift her up. In the last Dot Disclosure, we discussed sharing your Diagnosis with the glass is half full people. Speaking of glass half full, no doubt we will encounter those who do not see the brighter side of things. Remember the grumpy lady I sat next to in the infusion room on my first day of chemo? Ironically, Candy encountered a grumpy man on her first day of dialysis. He said in a loud voice, "I don't know why we are going through all this just to die", immediately heartbroken and afraid, my sweet Candy Cane cried. We talked on her ride home and I replied as only Iyanla Vanzant would, "Not on my watch." We're not having any of that Missy.

There was a Destiny waiting for her, and as one of her teammates, I was going to play my part to help her see it through. One day she called and thanked me for being there for her in the moments where her faith wavered, she admitted that she needed it, that was one of the most rewarding moments of our friendship, and guess what, like you reading this now, she is reading it too. You see, everyone loves and appreciates you during the good times when there are no worries or cares, it's those times of despair when you have nothing to give and all you can do is receive, ask, and depend on others, is when, in my opinion, you find out who your real friends are.

The Perfect Gift

Jayla, Candy's daughter, at the time was 14 years old, promised her mom on her 18th birthday she would give her the gift of donating her kidney. This touched Candy's heart and was a pivotal moment, and just like that, Everything is Perfect.

To transform this dream into a reality, there was hard work needed to be done. Candy must qualify for the transplant list, and that is not as simple as your daughter volunteering her kidney. My sweet Candy Cane did all the hard work, and in a year's time, she conditioned her mindset from sour to sweet, adhered to the strict diet from her Doctors, loss the necessary weight, ensured all her numbers, levels and bloodwork were exact and successfully completed steps 1 – 7 below:

1. Found a transplant hospital.

2. Ensured her Body Mass Index (BMI) was exact per the standards of the hospital.

3. Completed a series of 30 tests from head to toe to ensure everything in her body was functioning correctly.

4. Adhered to a mental evaluation with the hospital psychologist.

5. Completed a 6-week education series, learning the in's and out's of a transplant.

6. Qualified for the transplant list.

7. Found a donor who is willing to go through steps 1-6.

8. The other option if step 6 was not available was to wait on the list until her name came up with a perfect kidney match.

My girl got on that donor list!

Donors freely give their organs so humans can have a chance to continue living. Without that donation, a life is typically lost or severely shortened at the very least. Donors are vital! Donors save lives!

Dictionaries generally define a donor as (1) a person who donates something, especially money, to a fund or charity or (2) provides blood or transfusion of an organ and tissue for transplantation. Those in need of organ donations, like my friend Candy, understand the need and power of a donor. That same sentiment is true for those suffering from other diseases. A donor is especially important to a person who needs an organ to save their life. Donors are givers and their purpose is not fulfilled until they have a recipient, a person who is willing, open, and grateful to receive their blessing. For the purpose of this conversation, we are also defining Donors as (3) people who have so graciously decided to walk alongside us through our journey, show support, give love, and provide what we desperately need to heal, survive and thrive, even when we don't know that we need it.

Two Parts of a Blessing

It is more of a blessing to give than it is to receive. I think when it comes to Donors, it is important to realize that there are two parts of a blessing, the giver and the receiver. Without a receiver, the giver cannot be a blessing and without a giver, a receiver cannot be blessed. They are like a coin, with two sides to make it whole.

In full transparency, this was not the easiest part for me to grasp, which is why I am sharing it with you in this chapter. Remember in the dot Disclosure I shared the reason why it took so long for me to tell anyone is because I was embarrassed, and I didn't want to ask for help? Looking back, I know without a doubt, that if it were not for my Donors in Texas, who were my support system, I would have had to uproot my son and move back to Chicago where my family resides.

Those who know me know I am a giver, and I truly appreciate being able to give. Jayla, also a giver, gave to her mother a beautiful gift, the gift of life. Image how Jayla would have felt if for whatever reason her mother did not accept her gift.

I can easily think about what would have happened to me had I refused to receive the giving from my Donors. I want you to know that you don't have to be too proud on this journey. Pride comes before the fall, and we are not declaring destruction or falls on this journey. We are rising and walking towards our promised and expected end, full of hope and life. Be open to receiving the help you need. Do not miss out on blessings and shortchange someone else who can also be blessed by the opportunity to be a giver.

I can remember going through the Dots on my journey, in the beginning, not having shared much with the people who were going to support me. I was at Disclosure. If I did not shift, decide to do it differently, and kept being Ms. Independent, I would have cut myself off from the very thing I needed to survive and thrive, my Donors!

Disappointing: A Dot I Wish I Avoided

One of the people who was hurt by my hesitancy to disclose my Diagnosis was my mom. My mother and I have a deeply close relationship. We talk on the phone every day, sometimes several times, and we talk about everything. It was very hard keeping this from my mom, and in the end, she was the second person I told. I waited until I knew the diagnosis and treatment plan before I told her. Then, I could assure her that I was going to be okay and explain everything. It was the last week of September when we had the conversation. One of the first questions she asked was whether I knew on my birthday (the month prior), when she came to visit. I had known and I could hear in her voice, she was disappointed, because I didn't share it with her then.

No matter what the reason, she was disappointed and that made me cry. Once I explained the treatment plan, and when I would start chemo, she created a plan to fly out to be there for me and my son. Knowing this road was long, she was there every step of the way. Being who she is, my mom immediately began reminding me to keep a positive mindset and outlook, focus on healing, and be a contribution by giving and sharing.

Teamwork Makes the Dream Work

In that moment, I wasn't sure what teamwork looked like, so I held onto it with my eyes open, looking for opportunities. I did ask mom to hold off sharing with the family, until I got more detailed information. She agreed, was the gatekeeper, and when I felt the time was right she shared with family and friends. She asked if I had told my son and I had not yet; I wanted to tell her first. He and I sat down that evening and had a conversation.

My mom flew in a week before surgery and stayed with us for six weeks. For the next year, she visited twice a month, stayed for a week, and had her own key. This was a family effort, aka TEAM EFFORT! I love the acronym for TEAM that says, "Together Everyone Achieves More." This is so true. In the background, my dad had been in a bad car accident. He had multiple surgeries, was going through rehabilitation, and had doctor appointments several times a week. Every time my mom came to Texas to be with us, my "TT" came to the house to care for my dad. Again, a TEAM EFFORT! Auntie Diane came during the sixth week of my mother's stay for my surgery. We were all together for one week. My mom left and my aunt stayed another six weeks. She was so very loving, ensuring I took my medications on time, made it to doctor appointments, and helping around the house. She was also my partner in binge-watching Netflix. Many times, the pain medication would make me fall asleep and she would rewind the episodes that I missed. We had lots of fun talking, relaxing, and healing.

Then there was Linda Worden. A sweet and compassionate lady who I met while serving at church. She is a true example of agape love. She is kind, giving, creative, and has a great sense of style. She was immensely helpful after surgery. She coordinated a very special gift that warmed my heart and I still cherish it to this day. She collected sticky notes from about 200 women at church who wrote inspirational messages to me and placed them in a cute jar labeled *Patryce's Happiness Jar.* This was one of the gifts she brought to my home after surgery from the Women's Ministry. Once or twice a week, I'd pick out one of the notes from the jar and read the message. It made me feel like they were right there with me. After reading, I would return the note back to the jar and shake it up. After 3 years, I still haven't read them all. Sometimes, I reach inside and pull out a note previously read before. Other times, a brand-new sweet and refreshing note. Either way, the jar and lovely notes are heartfelt, thoughtful and a most delightful gift.

Lastly, I want to acknowledge my chemo buddies. My son Bakari Sheppard, Dawn Henry, Courtney Brooks, Torrie Diaz, and Hope Wharton were present at one time or another during my eight chemotherapy sessions, I cannot tell you what it was like to have buddies who were there to love on you when you are fighting for your life.

Learn the Easy Way

I want you to know that none of this is possible, if we do not disclose to anybody and if we do not humble ourselves to be on the receiving end of a blessing. If you remember nothing else about the last two chapters, remember that you need people. People tend to isolate themselves when they are sick. A huge part of the healing process starts from within, but it also includes others. Healing includes the social relationships and the people around us to keep us motivated and to fill in the everyday gaps, providing the necessary support we need.

I had to learn the hard way, but I don't want that for you. They say a hard head makes a soft butt. I don't want your butt being soft because of this. I prefer you get the assistance you need early so you focus your energy on the portion of the journey that only you can do!

Please release yourself to accept help. Not because of them because of you. It takes a tribe. As women, we wear so many hats and become independent, self-sufficient, and are stuck in a mode of doing things on our own. Allow yourself permission to ask. Everyone has a special skill and a heart to perform that task. Also, they love us and want to offer assistance in any way they can. It is our job to allow them access into our lives with the easiest route, so it is not taxing on them but helpful to us. The best way to do that is by creating a list of needs and asking friends to sign up. People are going to ask what they can do to help and it's so much easier when they are offered choices. Take the time on the front end to plan what those are. Allowing people who love you to help you is a gift to both of you.

To help support you in that, I've included a list of tasks and roles that my Donors helped me with, so you can have an idea when making your list.

Tasks/Roles of Your Donors, aka Dream Team

1. Meals.

2. Transportation (taking children to and from school and extracurricular activities).

3. Help with household chores (laundry, cleaning).

4. Rides to doctor appointments.

5. Chemo buddies (friends to accompany you to treatment).

6. Pet care (walking, groomers).

7. Visiting while sick.

8. Help with showers after surgery.

9. Prayer partners.

Additional Tips:

Create a list. A list allows people to pick what they are good at, so they feel competent in providing you the best care and support. You do not want someone who hates cooking responsible for making meals for you and your family!

Clear communication. There are a lot of moving parts so clear communication helps to minimize the confusion and frustration, ensuring the best care is available not just for you but for everyone who is a part of your healing team.

Assign a coordinator or point person. Like in basketball, there is only one ball, so everyone needs to have one direction and one goal. A point person or coordinator can help keep the peace and help things flow like clockwork. A perfect person for this is someone who probably does this in their day job, like an event planner or someone with management experience.

Provide time slots. The more specific you are, the better it is for everyone. This also helps people who are helping you avoid being overwhelmed. Hospitals do this with nurses to make sure they are fresh and not overworked. An overworked or overwhelmed person is not capable of giving you the best care even if they wanted to.

Before putting a bow on this dot, I want to address those who might not have the support I was blessed to have. Perhaps there is no team of aunties or maybe you and your mom are not so close. Where can you turn if that is you? There are numerous resources available to help women like us, who find themselves not having the support they need. You can find support groups by going to Google—yes, you can use Google for this, just don't look up medications, lol. The National Breast Cancer Foundation has resources that can connect you to local support groups as well. Hospitals provide resources to people like the nurse navigator or a case manager that you can lean on to get the support you need. Last but certainly not least, use social media and join a Facebook group. There are tons of Facebook groups that can provide you with the right kind of support and introduce you to resources that you may not know about.

Just know you are not alone and you can do this, as it is a part of your Development towards becoming exactly the person who you were destined to be. You got this. I know you do!

DOT #9: DEVELOPMENT

Circumstances create opportunities for ordinary people to do extraordinary things.

—*Patryce Sheppard*

Oh, my goodness, this quote speaks loudly to the Everything Is Perfect conversation from my mom. Outstanding! You see, looking back on the challenges of my breast cancer journey and days with ugly moments, I am grateful for every experience and circumstance, as they contributed to my growth in so many ways (inspired me to create a platform to support other diagnosed women, giving them tools, coaching, and a community of other powerful women, sharing significant journal and sticky note moments, spirit lifting affirmations, and fellowship with other pink sistas), moving me to grateful tears.

When you think you cannot survive another day, BUT YOU DO, realize how tough and resilient you are, knowing "you got this" you were built for this, you are a survivor, winner and powerful force being shaped and sculpted for bigger and better things, creating a better version of you.

Shifting your mindset to believing experiences are blessings, help ascend us to higher levels in personal Development and growth. Having a *doing it differently* mindset, plants high-yielding seeds for your caterpillar to butterfly metamorphosis, Winning!

I have blossomed to a woman, who understands and appreciates the power of sisterhood, loving friendships, transparency, and heartfelt sharing, with tons and tons of love. I am grateful for sticky notes and journals, because they connect the dots detailing your story with challenges, hallelujahs, and breakthroughs that build and bridge you from ordinary to doing extraordinary things. You were built for this, so do the work and win.

DOT #10: DESTINY

I am the first one to hold up my hand and say I have had so much help because of the position I am in. But I don't want to just take it and run, I want to use it to be an amplifier and magnifying glass for those who are not in this situation.

—*Robin Roberts*

Seems like only yesterday, with so many others praying for Robin Roberts as she openly shared her story. Now, here I am, hoping to make a difference at my Destiny.

My friend attended a Tony Robbins seminar, where she learned "the six human needs." Tony Robbins is a world-renowned motivational speaker and peak performance coach. He has helped people transition thoughts of suicide, compete at their highest level in sports, overcome addictions and more, by his no-nonsense style of coaching, so they release their power from within. What impressed my friend the most was the top two human needs, growth and Development.

We talked about growth and the process of *doing it differently* in dot #9: Development. Equally important is contribution, as it is a gift to give to others. It especially inspires and motivates when it comes from your personal scribblings on sticky notes and entries in your journal. It truly is better to give than receive. Like Robin Roberts, be a contribution and give.

Destiny is defined as, "a predetermined course of events often held to be by an inevitable power." Wow! Let me wrap my brain around "an inevitable power", so our journey was part of our Destiny, even before we were born. Right? No worries here, ladies, just live a fruitful life, the juice is worth the squeeze.

This is a call to lead by example, like when I powerfully declared my power back, after the grumpy lady's comment regarding me losing my beautiful curly hair, "cancer will NOT control me, I WILL CONTROL CANCER. I will lose my hair, by choosing to cut it myself, Period!

Now, that was a perfect example, right? What are yours? The world is counting on you to *doing it differently*, WE WERE BUILT FOR THIS, LET'S GO!!!

I am thankful you made it through the 10 dots and pray the information in this book blesses you. Again, thank you and, you got this!

CONCLUSION

Thank you for reading this book. Wherever you are on your breast cancer journey, please know you are in my prayers and I am proud of you. I know it is not easy, but you can and will get through this, just believe in yourself, do the work and win *doing it differently*. Remember, with this book you have tools, a community and coaching from me. I hope these resources powerfully support you from Discovery to Destiny, have an easier experience and give you hope, faith and positivity.

In Hindsight, as strange as this may sound, my diagnosis and going through the process to healing was a blessing. I am doing more purposeful work, my vision has expanded for helping women, my personal growth and Development is off the charts, and I have a beautiful a new friend, you!

After reading this book, please pass it on to someone as a blessing. Give a copy to a friend on their journey or join the support groups yourself and offer to be a donor (knowing it does not require an organ, just a gift of your time, sharing the lessons you learned, having a listening ear or simply, being a Netflix buddy). Everything is important and matters.

This book is what I wished for when I was diagnosis in 2017. Now that you have it in your hands, it's a blessing for you and a blessing for me. I pray it serves you.

I love you and may God continue to bless you,

Patryce

ACKNOWLEDGMENTS

Glory to God for strength, wisdom, and courage to endure, survive, and share my story, this story of inspiration and a shift in mindset with the world. I once understood, "exceedingly abundantly above all that we could ask or think" I now understand "according to the power that worketh in us." It is this experience that tested my faith, refined my character, and gave me a deeper understanding of grace and mercy.

My ancestors, great-grandmother Grammy, Grandpa Ben and Grandma Amy, Auntie Susie and Uncle B, Uncle Carlos, and Grandma Peggy, as I continue this journey of life, I'm so very grateful for everything that you taught me. Every lesson is ingrained in my spirit. Thank you for building a legacy of integrity and love in our family. Mom (Cheryl Sheppard-Rogers), Dad (William Rogers), brother (Patrick Sheppard) and my one and only son (Bakari Sheppard), thank you for being there with me every step of the way, the good, bad, and the ugly, not just through the breast cancer journey, but in life. And my aunties, Teresa Crittle and Diane Tillman, who were like older sisters as I grew up, your love and support through my journey is a direct reflection of the love you have shown all my life. To my cousins, family members, my church family, homegirls from Chicago who made it their business to be there for me, and the many others who passed through my life on my journey, I appreciate you!

There were and still are so many people who show their support. I can't name everyone—that's another book!—but I would like to acknowledge a few ladies and one gentleman who are the inspiration for Dot #8: Donors. LaToya Hill, Linda Worden, Stefanie Austin, and Cotis Evans: thank you for stepping in with your agape love, seeing a need, and going over and beyond to be sure that Bakari and I were taken care of. From the bottom of my heart, I thank you for taking charge to ensure my comfort and healing. To my chemo buddies, Bakari Sheppard, Dawn Henry, Torrie Diaz, Hope Wharton, and Courtney Brooks, Kevin McGowan (hands down the best barber), my childhood friends Nicol Benford, Ava Al-Amin, Candice Brandt, and Angelique Sankey, my "breast friends" Tamara Newborn, Gigi Vinique and Charmaine Henderson. Sonya "Sunny" Joseph for holding me accountable to staying focused and positive in those dark days, and Teresa Richards, Stephanie Powell, Ebony Humphrey, Monica Essue, and Thameetha Edwards there are no words to express my gratitude, hopefully thank you, Thank You, THANK YOU is appropriate.

In 2019, Janel Barksdale and I sat down to brainstorm this book. Thanks for planting seeds for this project. First Book Done family, Dr. Carl Stokes Jr., Connie Alleyne, Roderick Jefferson, Lyna Nyamwaya, Staci Scott, and Vania Swain, WE did it, WE are authors! Jessica Sipos, PhD, thank you for listening, hearing, relating, and editing with a different perspective. Geo Derice, my book doula, thank you for believing in me and reminding me time and time again that this book is relevant because it is a service.

Janelle Hail, founder of National Breast Cancer Foundation and Natasha Gayden, founder of Women with 20/20 Vision, thank you for walking alongside me through my journey, encouraging and acknowledging me, and giving me a platform to advocate for and share my message of education and awareness.

ABOUT THE AUTHOR

A native of Chicago, Patryce Sheppard changed careers in 2012 when she relocated to Texas and began working in insurance. In July of 2017, she was diagnosed with malignant breast cancer after discovering a suspicious lump while performing a self-breast exam. During her treatment and recovery, which included chemotherapy, a double mastectomy, radiation, and further therapy, Patryce depleted the six months of savings she had set aside for emergencies. She discovered her life insurance policy had living benefits— an accelerated death benefit rider—and received support that allowed her to continue her treatment without concern for bills and other expenses. She was able to concentrate on healing during the 18 months of treatment she received. The relief she experienced when she discovered the accelerated death benefit rider—and the time it afforded her to focus on healing and reflect on how she would like to contribute to the world after her recovery—led to a turning point in her life perspective and goals. She knew that when she was able to return to work, she wanted to help others experience what she was blessed to feel when she realized that, thanks to her insurance policy, she would be able to concentrate on her health and recovery without financial concerns.

After her recovery, she founded Faith in the Fight, an organization that supports and encourages women newly diagnosed with breast cancer, educates their loved ones on how to best support them in their treatment and recovery, and advocates for early detection of the disease.

Patryce has earned accolades for her dedication to activism on behalf of breast cancer support and awareness. In 2018, she received the Against All Odds award, the annual Survivor Award from Women with 20/20 Vision, and in 2019, she received the annual Rooted in the Community The Spirit of the National Breast Cancer Foundation. She was also honored as the 2019 Advocate of the Year by the National Breast Cancer Foundation. In addition, she holds speaking engagements across the country, sharing her story, and advocating for breast cancer awareness and the benefits and possibilities of insurance policies. In June 2021, she won the 2021 8% Nation Conference competition for public speaking. In July 2021, she released her first book, *Doing It Differently: An Empowering Approach to Thriving Through Breast Cancer,* with an accompanying workbook and journal.

Her philosophy of life and career is authenticity, sincerity, and caring. She is dedicated to her faith, passionate about helping others, and directs her charisma and charm toward an unwavering effort to see the best in a situation while being ready for the worst. Patryce believes in recognizing challenges, but keeping a steady focus on goals, aspirations, and destiny. This perspective guided her through a breast cancer diagnosis, treatment, and recovery, and is what guides her now in reaching, supporting, educating, and advocating for people who can benefit from her knowledge, experience, and passion.

Patryce resides with her 19-year-old son, Bakari, in Dallas, Texas.

Made in the USA
Coppell, TX
02 November 2021

65098341R00059